TURN THE OTHER CHEEK

PETER HORSLER

HANBURY PLAYS

KEEPER'S LODGE
BROUGHTON GREEN
DROITWICH
WORCESTERSHIRE WR9 7EE

BY THE SAME AUTHOR:-

One act
Published by Samuel French
   CHOICE
   CHRISTMAS INCORPORATED
   THE INTRUDERS
Published by Hanbury Plays
   CHRISTMAS WITH MIRABELLE

Full length
Published by Samuel French
   ON THE VERGE

FIRST PUBLISHED 1984

© Peter Horsler

ISBN 0 907926 34 7

CHARACTERS

Hester White
Joan Mann
Lettie White   – Hester's sister
Megan Woods – a gypsy woman
Merryl   – Megan's daughter

THE ACTION OF THE PLAY TAKES PLACE IN THE DINING ROOM OF THE WHITE'S FAMILY VILLA IMMEDIATELY FOLLOWING THE FUNERAL OF THEIR BROTHER, GEORGE.

THE ONLY DOOR WHICH LEADS INTO THE HALL IS UP LEFT. THERE IS A LARGE WINDOW IN THE UP-STAGE WALL WHICH HAS THE CURTAINS DRAWN THROUGHOUT THE ACTION SO THAT NO WINDOW FRAME OR BACKING IS NECESSARY. THE ROOM IS FURNISHED SIMPLY: THERE IS A SMALL DINING ROOM TABLE UP CENTRE WHICH IS PUSHED UP TO THE WALL BENEATH THE WINDOW AND WHICH HAS THREE PLAIN DINING CHAIRS PLACED AROUND IT ON ITS OPEN SIDES: A TELEPHONE TABLE WITH TELEPHONE STANDS UP RIGHT OF THE DINING TABLE: A SIDEBOARD RUNS ALONG THE UP-STAGE PART OF THE ROOM'S RIGHT WALL AND THERE IS AN EASY CHAIR DOWN LEFT BEHIND WHICH STANDS A PLAIN STANDARD LAMP. THE FURNISHING IS COMPLETED BY A SMALL OCCASIONAL TABLE SET BELOW THE EASY CHAIR.

WHEN THE CURTAIN RISES, THE STAGE IS EMPTY BUT IMMEDIATELY HESTER WHITE ENTERS FOLLOWED BY JOAN MANN AND LETTIE. HESTER AND LETTIE ARE BOTH DRESSED IN MOURNING; JOAN WEARS A SIMPLE BLACK ARM BAND AROUND THE SLEEVE OF HER SMART COSTUME.

Hester   Come in for a moment, Joan. They can't begrudge you a few more minutes surely after working for George for all those years. (TAKING OFF HER HAT AND COAT AND PLACING THEM ON THE TABLE AS SHE TALKS) It's not very comfortable in here, I'm afraid, but I can't face the other room just yet. (TO JOAN) Give me your coat.

Joan   It's all right. I musn't stay.

Hester   (INDICATING THE CHAIR DOWN LEFT) Well, anyway, sit down a moment.

Joan   (MOVING TO THE CHAIR DOWN LEFT AND SITTING) Just a moment then.

Lettie   Shall I hang the coats up, Hester ? We shan't be going out again today, shall we ?

Hester   If you must. Oh, and draw those wretched curtains. I can't bear all this gloom.

Lettie   I don't think we should, not just yet - not today.

Hester   George is dead, Lettie. Nothing will change that.

Lettie   Yes, but I wouldn't like people to think -

Hester   Leave them then. Joan, put that lamp on, will you ?

3

JOAN SWITCHES ON THE STANDARD LAMP. LETTIE PICKS UP
HESTER'S COAT AND HAT AND GOES OUT.

Hester (TURNING THE DOWNSTAGE TABLE CHAIR ROUND AND
MOVING IT TO RIGHT CENTRE AND THEN SITTING AS SHE
SPEAKS TO JOAN) You still have a job though ? Now George has gone
it doesn't mean - ?

Joan Yes, of course. That's one thing about the Council, they can always
use an experienced secretary.

Hester You'll find it strange though. I laid the table this morning for
three. Couldn't have been all honey, working for George.

Joan Not all the time, no. He was a hard man in a lot of ways, yet
there was another side.

Hester Shouldn't say it today, I suppose, but - well, tyrant might best
describe him.

Joan Oh, I thought perhaps at home with you two he might -

Hester Over-protective, shall we say ? But it made our lives very
restricted.

Joan Money, you mean ?

Hester My dear, as far as George was concerned, we couldn't
understand anything as complicated as money.

Joan You're all right, though ?

Hester Oh yes, according to Mr Wilkins, we shall be very comfortable:
several thousands in the current account apart from investments. Ironic
isn't it when he made us live like paupers - just look at the furniture in
this room. Well, I'm glad it doesn't mean you're out of a job.

Joan A change may do me good. I'll tell you one thing - I'm not
sorry this will mean the end of the gypsy campaign.

LETTIE ENTERS.

Lettie They're all put away properly. (MOVING THE LEFT DINING CHAIR
DOWN STAGE TO LEFT OF HESTER'S CHAIR AND SITTING) I can't
bear clothes left around the house, can you, Joan ?

Joan My family could take a few lessons from you, Lettie.

Hester Always was the tidy one - hates muddle. You think they'll take a
softer line with the gypsies from now on ?

Joan Well, it was George's obsession.

Lettie You talking of gypsies, reminds me. Did you see that dreadful pair
at the funeral ? You know, the old woman and her daughter, the
one whose little boy was run over.

Hester No, were they ?

Lettie Standing up the hill, in the old part, under the fir trees.

Joan I saw two women. Is that who they were ?

Lettie Yes, I'm sure. Don't you remember, their pictures were in all the
papers ?

Hester Poor wretches.

Joan The last people to pay respect to George, I should have thought.

Hester Perhaps they came to curse.

Lettie Hester ! How can you say such a thing ?

Hester Well, they had good reason to hate George.

Lettie He was only doing his job. Somebody had to stop them putting their
dirty caravans where decent people live. It wasn't his fault that the boy
was run over when they towed them out. That sort don't look after their
children, let them run wild in rags, then complain when something
happens. I've no patience. Anyway, some people were grateful for what he
did. Look at that bottle of sherry.

4

Hester Sherry, of course. I'd forgotten that. (RISING) Will you have a glass, Joan ? I'm sorry we haven't offered you anything but there being no family - well, I didn't think - I hope the others won't think I'm awful.

Joan They had to go straight back anyway. I'm sure they wouldn't have expected -

Hester (CROSSING TO THE SIDEBOARD) Well, you'll have a glass ?

Joan I ought to be - oh, all right, if it will make you feel better.

Hester Didn't occur to me. You see, we never drink - any of us. This bottle was a gift.

Lettie From someone to thank George for clearing up the gypsies.

Hester (TAKING A GLASS FROM OUT OF THE SIDEBOARD AND POURING OUT A DRINK) He didn't drink either, though he did have one glass the night before he died. Said he felt a bit low, thought it might perk him up.

Lettie I think I'd like one, Hester. Today has been rather a trial.

Hester You, Lettie ? Wouldn't tea be -

Lettie No, I'll try a glass of that.

Hester Very well, dear. You won't like it though. (SHE POURS A SECOND GLASS)

Joan Only fit for guests, is it ?

Hester I didn't mean - I think it is a good one or George wouldn't have - not that I know anything about it. Never touched alcohol, never shall; though I don't mind others.

Joan Even Lettie ?

Hester She's old enough to make her own decisions. (COMING AND GIVING A GLASS TO JOAN) There we are. I don't suppose George would have approved. (TAKING A GLASS UP TO LETTIE) And I know he wouldn't of you - still, we don't have to consider that now, do we ? (SHE SITS RIGHT OF LETTIE)

Joan What was the verdict at the inquest ? I never did hear.

Hester Cardiac arrest - that's all. The doctor was very puzzled.

Joan He didn't have heart trouble, did he ?

Hester George ? No, strong as a horse - or so we thought. Remember how he manhandled those gypsies ?

Lettie They tried all the tests though. They were very thorough. Each organ was -

Hester All right, Lettie. You needn't go into details.

Joan And they found nothing ?

Hester No - it seemed his heart just stopped.

Lettie (SOBBING) Poor, dear George.

Joan Well, at least he didn't suffer. (DRAINING HER GLASS AND PLACING IT ON THE SMALL TABLE) I really must go. (RISING) If you have any problems, if you need a friend, don't hesitate to ring. It's the same department but Mr Morton's office. Just ask for extension 61.

Hester (RISING) Thank you for coming, dear.

Joan Least I could do. Well, goodbye. Goodbye, Lettie.

Lettie (STILL SOBBING) Goodbye.

Hester (EASING TO DOOR) Mr Morton's office ?

Joan Yes, don't worry. I'll see myself out. (EXIT)

Hester (COMING DOWN TO LETTIE'S RIGHT) Pull yourself together, Lettie. There really is nothing to cry about. (PUTTING HER ARM ROUND HER) Come and sit in the easy chair. (SHE HELPS HER UP AND GUIDES HER TO THE CHAIR DOWN LEFT) I'll light a fire in the lounge after tea.

5

Lettie Not in there, where George - I couldn't, not yet.

Hester (PUTTING HER LEFT ARM ON LETTIE'S RIGHT SHOULDER) We're just being silly. George has gone and we've got to live without him and - if you think about it - it's going to be a much better life.

Lettie How can you, Hester - your own brother ?

Hester Nevertheless it's true. (SITTING ON CHAIR LEFT CENTRE) Look, we'll use some of that money for a world cruise. How would you like that ?

Lettie Doesn't seem right somehow - George's money.

Hester It's ours now; he has no use for it.

THE FRONT DOORBELL RINGS.

Hester Who can that - ? Joan must have forgotten something.

Lettie I'm sorry, Hester. I'm being silly again. I'm just not strong like you.

THE BELL RINGS AGAIN.

Lettie (RISING) I'll go.

Hester No, dear, you sit -

Lettie I musn't give way. I'll go !

Hester All right, dear. I expect it's only Joan.

LETTIE EXITS.

Hester (CALLING TO HER) I'll lay the tea, dear. (SHE CROSSES TO THE SIDEBOARD, OPENS A DRAWER, TAKES OUT A CLOTH AND SPREADS IT OVER THE TABLE)

Lettie (NIPPING IN AND CLOSING THE DOOR QUICKLY BEHIND HER) It's those gypsies !

Hester What ?

Lettie The two at the cemetery. They want to talk to you - very important, they say.

Hester Well, you'd better ask them in.

Lettie In ? Gypsies ?

Hester We can't talk in the street.

Lettie But they're - well, so dirty. I mean they're gypsies.

Hester I know. You said they were. Ask them in.

Lettie (INDICATING THE DINING CHAIRS) Have you something to cover these ? I mean, what would George - ?

Hester Ask them in !

LETTIE SLIPS OUT OF THE DOOR. HESTER MOVES THE CHAIR RIGHT OF THE TABLE TO DOWN RIGHT. AS SHE DOES SO, LETTIE RETURNS FOLLOWED BY MEGAN AND MERRYL.

Lettie This is my sister, Miss Hester.

Hester How do you do, Mrs ...

Megan Woods, lady - Woods.

Hester Mrs Woods.

Megan (INDICATING MERRYL) Me daughter, Merryl.

Hester (INDICATING THE TWO CHAIRS CENTRE) Won't you sit down ?

MEGAN AND MERRYL SIT, EYING HESTER WARILY.

Hester (AFTER A PAUSE) You've met my sister, Lettie ?

Megan (NODDING IN LETTIE'S DIRECTION) Her what let us in ?

LETTIE MOVES DOWN CAUTIOUSLY TO THE ARMCHAIR DOWN LEFT, KEEPING HER EYES ON THE TWO GYPSIES AS SHE DOES SO.

Hester (MOVING TO CHAIR DOWN RIGHT AND SITTING) Now, Mrs Woods, what can I do for you ?

Megan You seen us, didn't yer ?

Hester At the cemetary ? My sister did, yes.

Merryl Never meant nothing 'gainst you.

Megan Only him, your dinlo brother. We called the rider for him.

Hester Dinlo ? Rider ?

Merryl The rider got him.

Hester What is all this ? What are you trying to say ?

Megan We done it for her little charo. *chikno*

Merryl My chikno.

Hester Chikno ?

Megan Her kid. We killed him for her chikno. *Kid*

Hester Killed ? Who ?

Merryl Him what done it - the council man.

Lettie George ?

Hester (JUMPING UP) George ! You killed George ?

LETTIE SCREAMS, HALF RISES FROM HER CHAIR, THEN COLLAPSES SOBBING.

Hester (CROSSING TO UP RIGHT OF LETTIE) Nonsense. George died of natural causes. Now look, Mrs Woods, we don't believe in curses and things like that. I know you hated my brother and I don't blame you, but he's dead now. (CROSSING ABOVE CHAIR TO HER SEAT RIGHT) Think you were responsible if you like, if it's any comfort, but nothing is going to bring your grandson back. We must try to forget the past and start again. (SHE SITS) Only you can do that: if you forgive, we may all learn to live together.

Lettie What have they to forgive ? We've never done anything to -it wasn't George's fault, if that's what you mean. You can't expect people to put up with their mess; living like animals !

Megan What do you know ?

Merryl Me daia's varda's cleaner than this here house o' yourn, it is.

Hester (RISING) Lettie, how could you ? She's right - we know nothing about the way they live.

Lettie (CROSSING TO HESTER'S LEFT) Varda ? I don't even understand what she's saying - she can't even speak English.

Hester Varda is Romany for home, I believe. She means her caravan. We should respect other people's traditions not condemn them for being different. (TO MEGAN) Perhaps we might visit your varda, Mrs Woods, then my sister could see.

Lettie I couldn't. What would people say ! I've seen where they live - the mess, broken bits of cars, smelly fires, filthy washing.(CROSSING BACK TO ARMCHAIR) You'll go on your own, Hester White. Nothing would induce me to. (SHE SITS)

Merryl (RISING) Dardi ! Filthy Geyri ! (SPITTING AT LETTIE) All the same, ain't you ?

Megan (DRAWING MERRYL BACK TO HER SEAT) Hush, chikni ! Let your daia speak. The lady's right: (HESTER SITS) everything's filthy, dirty mud and mess, nothing but mud and mess. Not like we want,lady, though, not like the old days. It's not our way, lady, we're not didikais. Romanies keep everything clean and bright, not like poshrat gypsies. When I was a little chari, we had a horse and our varda. We travelled, we worked, we rested. The givengros - sorry, lady, - the farmers, were our friends and pleased to see us. Now all is changed; nobody wants us; we are moved on, have nowhere to stay, no work, only collecting scrap. Nobody wants our pegs and no one believes in our dukkering.

Kid

7

Hester Dukkering ?

Merryl The fortune telling, crossing our palms with silver, Mrs. (TO MEGAN) You want that back, daia ? "Thank you, lady, thank you, mister". You want that ?

Megan The tree can't go back to the nut, but I want new ways, better ways for our people. (TURNING TO HESTER) You could help, lady.

Hester Me ? I don't see -

Merryl Owe us - my little chikno.

Megan You're rich lady.

Hester Well, not rich but -

Merryl Not poor like us.

Hester Well, no. I don't know.

Merryl A bit of land, Mrs, all we want - a bit of land.

Hester The Council -

Megan (SPITTING) Dardi Gaujos ! Do nothing for us !

Merryl Buy us a bit of land, Mrs, and you'll see.

Megan You'll see how we want to live, lady, no didikai dump.

Lettie (RISING) Buy you land ? You must be mad if you think -

Hester (CROSSING TO HER RIGHT) Just a minute, Lettie. We have George's money now.

Lettie It's our money. You can't think of spending it on -

Hester We don't need it and George - well, he owes these people something

Lettie He'd turn in his grave ! How could you be so stupid, Hester ? Can't you see they're just scroungers, beggars ? What have they ever done to deserve anything; they contribute nothing. Vultures - that's what they are, picking over George's bones ! You can't give them money; I won't let you !

Merryl You owe us, Mrs.

Lettie We owe you nothing.

Megan Her chikno died; he done it.

Lettie George only did what any decent man would do. He wasn't a spineless scrounger, no, and people looked up to him for it. They were grateful. (INDICATING THE WINE ON THE SIDEBOARD) Someone even sent him that because they admired his strength. He knew what you were all right. (SHE SINKS UNSTEADILY INTO THE CHAIR) Oh, dear.

Megan The rider took him.

Merryl And we sent the rider.

Hester (CROSSING BEHIND GYPSIES TO MEGAN'S RIGHT) Please, Mrs Woods, no more of this nonsense. If Lettie will not sign for the money, I'm afraid I can't help.

Megan Who drunk it then ?

Hester Drunk ?

Merryl (POINTING TO THE BOTTLE) The wine. Did he have that much ?

Hester Well, what has that ... ?

Megan How we done it.

Lettie (STRUGGLING TO GET UP) The sherry ! They poisoned the sherry ! Oh, my God, I drank it. Do something, Hester, get a doctor ! (SHE FALLS BACK INTO THE CHAIR, SOBBING)

Hester (RUSHING TO HER AND PUTTING HER ARM ROUND HER) Don't be silly, Lettie. George died of natural causes. We know he wasn't poisoned. (TO MEGAN) How dare you come here to frighten us ? We've never harmed you ?

Megan Little fishes get caught in big fish's nets.

Hester Get out of my house or I'll call the police ! It's all right, Lettie, don't let them scare you. (CROSSING TO THE PHONE) I'll call the doctor You've had a nasty fright - that's all, a nasty fright.

Merryl Call the gavvers and the rider gets her.

Lettie Make them go ! Please, make them go !

Hester (COMING DOWN TO MEGAN'S RIGHT) All right, you've had your revenge. Now go !

Megan (RISING) Then, lady, she'll be dead.

Merryl (RISING) No gaujo drabengro knows a cure. Only daia can save her now.

Hester Stop all this nonsense and get out !

Megan Nonsense is it, lady ? Well, tell her to move her arms.

Merryl Always arms first, ain't it daia ?

Lettie (STRUGGLING TO MOVE HER ARMS) They have - I can't, I can't ! They have poisoned me !

Hester (RUSHING ACROSS TO LETTIE'S RIGHT)   It's suggestion, that's all, Lettie - the power of suggestion. You can move your arms - you can ! We know George wasn't poisoned - the tests !

Megan Never leaves no trace. Tell her to move her legs.

Lettie (STRUGGLING TO MOVE HER LEGS) They've gone too - it's true, it's true ! Help me, Hester !

Merryl Our people know from way back.

Megan We can cure and we can kill.

Hester They're lying, darling, they're lying !

Merryl Show her the cure, daia, or the rider will win.

MEGAN MOVES DOWN RIGHT, LOOKS AT HESTER AND TAKES OUT A SMALL BOTTLE OF CLEAR FLUID FROM UNDER HER SHAWL.

Megan (HOLDING UP THE BOTTLE) A few drops, lady, a few drops, all she needs.

Hester (RUSHING ACROSS AND TRYING TO TAKE THE BOTTLE FROM HER) Give it me ! I don't care if it is your accursed psychology - let me give some !

Megan (REFUSING TO LET GO OF THE BOTTLE) A few drops, lady, for a piece of land.

Hester Yes, all right ! Just give her a few drops !

Megan She'll have to sign.

Hester Give me the bottle. She'll agree !

Merryl How do we know ?

Hester Our word, you can trust our word.

Merryl (SPITTING) Geyri's word !

Hester I promise, I swear - tell them, Lettie !

Lettie Never ! I'd rather die than give them a penny. Thieves, blackmailers, that's what you are !

Hester (MOVING SWIFTLY TO LETTIE AND FALLING ON HER KNEES BEFORE HER) Lettie, please, for my sake !

Lettie Our money for these filthy - I can't, I won't !

Merryl (MOVING DOWN TO MEGAN'S LEFT) Let the rider take her, daia, the dirty Gaujo !

Hester They've done something to you, Lettie; if it's not poison, it's hypnotism or some power we don't know about. They're the only ones who can help. Give them the money, it's not important. We never needed - please, Lettie !

Megan A bit of land, lady, all we ask. Give our people a chance to show we ain't didikais. We don't want no trouble - just to live, all we want.

Lettie (BEGINNING TO SOB) Why should I ? All my life, George has never- so many things I wanted and now you want it all. Take it from me - what right have you ?

HESTER RISES AND LOOKS IMPLORINGLY AT MEGAN AND MERRYL.

Merryl Dirty Gaujo, treat us like dirt; take our land; kill our chiknos.

Lettie   Your land ? You! Scavengers, parasites ! You don't belong here, don't own anything, don't deserve anything ! Get out of our country ! (STRUGGLES TO MOVE BUT CANNOT) Take your potions and poisons ! Go away, we don't want you !

Merryl (CROSSING TO LEFT CENTRE) Your land ? We have rights, Geyri !

Megan   Our father's father, his father's father roamed this land. Our vardas have seen acorns turn to oaks; ~~those same oaks shed acorns and again turn to oaks.~~ *again & again*

Merryl   It is our land, Geyri - not to buy and sell, but walk on its earth and breathe its air.

Hester   Please, Lettie, let them have the money. (INDICATING BOTTLE HELD BY MEGAN) Only, drink the antidote !

Megan   Or go with the rider.

Lettie   George knew what you were - he was right: a black cancer, destroying our country. He hated you, hated everything about you: the way you live, the way you look, the way you speak. And I hate you ! I won't give you my money to buy our land, I won't ! I won't ! (SHE BEGINS TO CHOKE) Hester, get a doctor, quick ! (SHE LOSES CONSCIOUSNESS)

HESTER STARES AT HER, THEN DARTS ACROSS TO MEGAN.

Merryl   (BACKING TO MEGAN) The rider is near.

Hester   (TRYING TO WRESTLE THE BOTTLE AWAY FROM MEGAN) Let go, do you hear ! You'll get your money; just let her live !

MEGAN LETS GO OF THE BOTTLE AND HESTER RUSHES TO LETTIE, PULLING OUT THE CORK AS SHE DOES SO.

Hester   All right, darling, drink this and you'll soon feel - (SHE FREEZES, STARING AT LETTIE. THEN, AFTER A PAUSE, SPEAKS SOFTLY TO HERSELF) My God ! (SHE LIFTS ONE OF LETTIE'S EYELIDS) She's - she's dead ! (THE BOTTLE OF ANTIDOTE DROPS FROM HER FINGERS)

Megan   (MOVING SWIFTLY TO THE ARMCHAIR TO PEER AT LETTIE) No, lady, she ain't, ain't possible. (SHRINKING BACK LEFT) Moshto, moshto, the rider's been !

Hester   (TURNING TO FACE THEM) Murderers ! You've murdered my sister!

Megan   (CRINGING AND BACKING DOWN RIGHT) No, lady, no, lady. (QUIETLY TO MERRYL) Arivell, the devil, Arivell.

Merryl   Arivell, daia, Arivell.

Hester   Murderers ! (CROSSING QUICKLY TO THE PHONE) The police !

Megan   (RUSHING UP TO HESTER'S LEFT AND CLUTCHING HER ARM) Not the gavvers, lady, no, lady, we never done it !

MERRYL, WHO HAS TAKEN A LONG KNIFE FROM UNDER HER SKIRT, RUSHES UP TO HESTER'S RIGHT, GRABS HER RIGHT HAND WITH HER LEFT AND RAISES THE KNIFE TO STRIKE.

Megan   ~~Chavain !~~ *Dait*

Merryl   (PAUSING) We'll be lelled !

Megan   Kill her and all our people will be hunted like the fox.

MERRYL SLOWLY LOWERS THE KNIFE.

Hester   At least your mother has some sense. ~~Now, let go of my hand or it will be the worse for you !~~

MERRYL RELEASES HER HAND.

Megan   We never done it, lady, we never -

Hester   You killed my sister one way or another and you're going to pay, you and all your sort.

10

Megan We never, lady, we never meant -

Merryl Accident, Mrs, accident, her heart -

Hester (TO MEGAN) Let go of my arm, do you hear !

Megan Please, lady, the gavvers - we'll get the blame. Gavvers hate travellers. There'll be figh ing - people will think - children will die.

Merryl Like my chikno.

Megan Blood, lady, blood will run, more than ever was. (INDICATING THE BOTTLE) Water, all it was. We never sent no wine.

Merryl Trying yer, we was. Never meant no harm.

Megan Only the land, all we wanted - the land for our people. Don't do it, lady, don't make the hate no worse.

Hester But you killed her.

Megan Never meant it, lady.

Merryl We're sorry, Mrs. Weren't to know, was we ?

Hester You frightened her to death.

Megan Without the land, our people will be doomed; nowhere to go.

Merryl Pushed around; cursed and kicked.

Megan Maimed and killed.

Hester I don't know - I just can't -

Megan Won't bring her back, lady. Little chavis killed. (LETS GO OF HESTER'S ARM)

Merryl Like my chikno.

Megan What for but revenge, lady ?

Hester (BREAKING AWAY FROM THEM AND MOVING TO THE CHAIR DOWN RIGHT) I don't know, I don't know ! (SITS WITH HER HEAD IN HER HANDS)

THE TWO GYPSIES MOVE ACROSS TO BEHIND THE CHAIRS CENTRE, THEIR EYES WATCHING HER, WAITING. THERE IS A LONG PAUSE.

Hester (WITH SUDDEN RESOLVE) You're right, of course. It will only add misery to misery. Your people have suffered so much. (RISING AND MOVING TOWARDS MEGAN) This land - what will it cost ?

Megan Twenty thousand but we could manage -

Hester No, you need a new beginning. There may be enough, from what Mr Wilkins said - I don't know, but you shall have it all. Poor George (CROSSING TO ABOVE LETTIE AND LOOKING DOWN ON HER - PAUSE) and Lettie (PULLING HERSELF TOGETHER) but it's all mine now. Sit down a moment and I'll phone - see what there is. (CROSSING TO ABOVE MEGAN AND MERRYL) Oh dear, I hope Mr Wilkins won't think - well, never mind.

MEGAN AND MERRYL SIT ON THE CHAIRS CENTRE.

Megan We're sorry, lady. Never should have done it, only we was desperate see, and your brother -

HESTER (MOVING TO DOWN RIGHT CENTRE) I can understand how you felt about George but trying to scare money out of us - well, you couldn't foresee the consequences - but -

Merryl We know, lady, we know.

Hester Yes, I can see you do. Would you mind if I put a notice in the paper, making it a bequest from George ?

Megan Bequest, lady ?

Hester A gift, a present. It might help if people thought that George had had a change of heart; might make them see their prejudice for what it is.

Megan All the same to us, lady, long as we has the land.

Hester (CROSSING TO LETTIE AND LOOKING DOWN ON HER) Very well, if the doctor is satisfied, I'll, say that Lettie had a seizure - the shock of George's death perhaps. (TURNING TO THEM) Nobody need know you've

11

been here. Now go - you'll get your money.

THE GYPSIES MOVE UP LEFT TOWARDS THE DOOR. THE PHONE RINGS.

Hester   (CROSSING TO THE PHONE) No, wait a minute. I need to know where to find you. You can't come here again. (PICKING UP THE PHONE) Hello, yes it is. Who did you say ? Mr Morton, oh yes. Bad news ? Joan ! Yes, she was here - yes, a good friend - why has something happened ? Car crash ? Dead. (MEGAN AND MERRYL EXCHANGE GLANCES) How did it happen ? I see, lost consciousness at the wheel - are they sure about that ? (SHE LOOKS AT THE TWO GYPSIES WHO ARE STARING AT HER WITH AN EXPRESSION OF HORROR) Yes, thank you - a great shock. Yes, I will later. No, I'd rather know, thank you. (SHE REPLACES THE RECEIVER SLOWLY, STILL STARING AT MEGAN AND MERRYL)

Megan   No, lady, no, we never, lady, we never !

Hester   George, Lettie and now Joan, poisoned. You've killed them all. (TAKING A STEP TOWARDS THEM) You are murderers !

Merryl   Not murder, not us, Mrs, not us !

Megan   (CRINGING AND MOVING TOWARDS HESTER) Never sent no wine, lady.

Merryl   Just saw it there, made it up to get the -

Megan   For the land, lady, see, for the land.

HESTER SUDDENLY PICKS UP THE PHONE AND STARTS TO DIAL FRANTICALLY. MERRYL DARTS FORWARD AND CLAMPS HER HAND OVER THE PHONE REST, DEPRESSING THE REST BAR.

Hester   (SUPPRESSING A SCREAM) Now you will have to kill me ! (SHE CRINGES AWAY. MEGAN BARS HER WAY TO THE DOOR)

Merryl   (DRAWING OUT HER KNIFE) No other way, Mrs, no other way.

Hester   Then you'll never get the money, never own your own land.

Megan   (TO MERRYL) Chavain, cheri ! (TO HESTER) I swear by Moshta, lady, the wine was good.

Hester   So you admit you sent it now.

Megan   To frighten - not to kill.

Merryl   An old trick, Mrs, the cure's just water see, but they believe -

Hester   You're liars ! It must be poisoned: George, Lettie and now Joan. Kill me ! Go on, kill me, but the police will get you in the end.

MERRYL BEGINS TO MOVE TOWARDS HER, READY TO STRIKE WITH THE KNIFE. MEGAN RUSHES BELOW CHAIRS TO SIDEBOARD AND PICKS UP THE BOTTLE OF WINE.

Megan Chavi!

MERRYL HESITATES.

Megan   Good wine, lady, see good wine.

SHE PULLS OUT THE CORK, RAISES THE BOTTLE TO HER LIPS AND PRETENDS TO DRINK. MERRYL MOVES TOWARDS HER AS IF TO STOP HER.

Megan   (TO MERRYL) Hush, mandi kom ! (TO HESTER) See, the wine is good.

Hester   But Lettie, Joan ?

Megan   The way of O puro being, lady.

Merryl   God's work, Mrs - God's work.

Hester   It can't just be a coincidence, it can't. You can't expect me to believe -

Megan O puro being - who knows, lady ?

Merryl His ways are strange.

Megan Stranger than the moon in a dark pool.

Hester (MOVING DOWN LEFT, SPEAKING TO HERSELF) There must be some reason, an explanation. If not the wine, what ?

Megan Not the wine.

Merryl Would daia drink poison, Mrs ?

Hester I don't know. (TURNING TO MEGAN) No, of course she wouldn't. But did she drink it ? She raised the bottle but - sit down ! Both of you, sit down'.

WATCHING HER WARILY, THEY BOTH SIT ON THE CHAIRS CENTRE. HESTER, KEEPING HER EYES ON THEM, MOVES ABOVE THEM TO THE SIDEBOARD AND TAKES OUT TWO NEW GLASSES WHICH SHE FILLS WITH WINE.

Hester (GIVING THE GLASSES TO MEGAN AND MERRYL) Let me see you both drink it then, if it's not poisoned.

MEGAN AND MERRYL EXCHANGE GLANCES.

Megan (RAISING HER GLASS) O puro Romany. (DRAINS HER GLASS)

Merryl (HESITATING A MOMENT, THEN RAISING HER GLASS) O puro daia (SHE DRINKS)

Hester (AFTER A PAUSE) So, you did tell the truth then. It wasn't the wine. (TAKES THE GLASSES AND RETURNS THEM TO THE SIDEBOARD MEGAN AND MERRYL CONTINUE TO STARE FIXEDLY IN FRONT OF THEM.) I feel very embarrassed. You must understand - the shock. When I heard about Joan, what else could I think ? You said it was poisoned - killed George. (TO RIGHT CENTRE) I'm sorry I - but you did threaten me with a knife.

Merryl The gavvers, Mrs - all travellers are frighted by the gavvers. Always been hard on us, they have.

Hester The police, yes. Well, they have to carry out their orders. I mean it's not what they wish: it's men like Geor-

Megan Our people always suffered, lady; your man was just the last. It's in the Geyro blood, always in the blood.

Merryl Hate for the Romany.

Hester (SITTING ON CHAIR DOWN RIGHT) I know your kind have been persecuted over the years, but you're not alone: it's happened to all minority groups who stand out as being different. It's fear, you see, fear fanned by ignorance. People cannot blame themselves for their misfortunes, so they use you and people like you. Their troubles all come from you and not from them. But things are changing slowly as -

Merryl Gaujos do not change, dardi Gaujos !

Megan Hush, chikni, mandi kom.

Hester I don't blame you for hating us, but hate will only create more hate.

Megan The wheel of hate.

Hester (TURNING AWAY FROM MEGAN TO SPEAK OUT FRONT) Going round endlessly. You hate us for what we've done to you and (TURNING TO HER) when we try to make amends, through your hate, see malice where none is meant. (TURNING AWAY AGAIN) Rebuffed, our good intentions turn to hate and so it goes on from generation to generation.

Merryl No gaujo ever meant to help the Romanies.

Hester (MOVING SWIFTLY ABOVE THE GYPSIES TO MERRYL'S LEFT) Yes, yes, some understand and try to right the wrongs of the past, but it can only happen if you forgive. We have to start again, you have to forget past ills: we must overide our prejudice. It will take time, but only you can make it happen.

Megan   Lady, you are right. We Romanies must look for the good; ignore the bad. (TO MERRYL) Chikni, mark my words, the future is with you. It will be hard, but it is the only way. (HER HEAD DROPS TO HER CHEST)

Merryl   Daia ?

Megan   It is nothing, chikni, I am too long away from the moving air.

Merryl   A cup of water, Mrs, for my daia ? She's not used to houses.

Hester   A glass of water, of course. I'll get her one. I won't be a a moment. (EXIT)

Merryl   Quick, daia, the cure !

MERRYL SEARCHES FRANTICALLY ON THE FLOOR FOR THE DROPPED BOTTLE.

Megan   Hurry, chikni, I hear the rider.

Merryl   (FINDING THE BOTTLE ABOVE THE ARMCHAIR) I have it, daia ! (STILL KNEELING, SHE PICKS IT UP AND HOLDS IT TO THE LIGHT) Daia, all is gone !

Megan   Then the rider will come.

Merryl   (RISING AND MOVING TO HER LEFT AND TRYING TO MAKE HER STAND) No, daia, we must hurry back to the varda, find some more

Megan   There is no time, mandi kom, the rider has won.

Merryl   (IMPLORINGLY) No, no, daia, we must try !

Megan   (DRAWING HER DOWN TO SIT) Hush, chikni, come sit, keep still or you will bring the rider quicker than need be.

Merryl   But, daia -

Megan   The land for our people - the Romany is all. We called the rider, we are to blame. The money - then take me out to die under the open sky. She must never know. We'll meet the rider together, and together go to find your little chikno.

HESTER ENTERS, CARRYING A GLASS OF WATER AND CROSSES ABOVE CHAIRS TO MEGAN'S RIGHT.

Hester   Here we are. (GIVES GLASS TO MEGAN, WHO SIPS IT SLOWLY)

Merryl   Lady, the land ?

Hester   Yes, it shall be a gift from my people to yours - a start.

Merryl   How, lady, how ?

Hester   Well, it will take time, of course, to settle George's affairs, and then (LOOKING SADLY AT LETTIE) there's poor Lettie. I'll let you know

Merryl   But you will never find us.

Megan   Wanderers, travellers, always journeying until we get our land.

Merryl   But there is a man, lady, a poshrat.

Hester   Poshrat ?

Megan   Half-gypsy.

Merryl   He knows us, lady, looks after us - he's the travellers' man of law.

Hester   A lawyer.

Merryl   Yes.

Hester   Where will I find him ?

Merryl   I'll write his name. (LOOKS FOR SOMETHING TO WRITE ON)

Megan   She can write, my Merryl. Not like her poor daia. Hurry, mandi kom, I want to feel the wind on my face again.

Hester   (MOVING TO THE SIDEBOARD) There's a pad in the drawer. (LOOKS IN DRAWER AND PRODUCES A WRITING PAD) Should be a pen Yes, here we are. (BRINGS THE PAD AND PEN TO MERRYL WHO LABORIOUSLY WRITES ON IT) I suppose I can trust this man ?

14

Megan As winter follows summer, lady, as trees bud in the spring he'll be true to the Romanies.

Hester You know the land you want ?

Megan The old quarry, lady, off the Meldon Road. There's a little stream there and room for twenty vardas.

Hester I know, George wanted the council to buy it for a caravan park. Well, so it shall be, though not quite as he intended. (TAKES THE PAD FROM MERRYL AND PLACES IT ON SIDEBOARD) Trust me, Mrs Woods, You'll see your land before a year is out. (COMING BACK TO RIGHT OF MEGAN) Now, would you like a cup of tea before you go ?

Merryl (RISING) No, thank you, lady, we have a long journey to make. (HELPS MEGAN TO HER FEET)

Megan A long, dark journey.

Hester Oh, it won't be dark for a while yet. It's the curtains, you see.

Megan Thank you, lady.

Hester (OFFERING HER HAND) I hope we meet again, Mrs Woods. This is a new beginning.

Megan An end and a beginning.

Hester Yes, I hope your troubles are over. (OFFERING HAND TO MERRYL) Goodbye, Merryl. I hope you'll soon think better of us - what did you call us ? Gaujos ?

Merryl I'll not hate any more, lady, not any more.

Hester (CONDUCTING THEM TO DOOR) I don't think it's raining and you should get back before dark.

THEY GO OUT AND WE HEAR THE FRONT DOOR OPEN.

Hester (OFF) Goodbye then.

THE FRONT DOOR CLOSES AND HESTER RETURNS.

Hester (LOOKING AT LETTIE FROM DOOR, THEN COMING DOWN TO ABOVE HER) How could I think of their problems with you lying there ? Oh, my poor, poor Lettie. Forgive me, but I had to right the wrong. I know you understand really, in spite of what you said. (SITS IN CHAIR UP CENTRE, HER HEAD IN HER HANDS) What will I do without you and George ? A few days ago everything was as it's always been and now - it's all been too much. I'm not myself - how could I let you lie there while I talked of new beginnings ? There's no one I can turn to - poor, dear Joan has gone too - no one, no one. (SOBS THEN PULLS HERSELF TOGETHER) No, I musn't give way. This has been a test. I know what I must do - I've been chosen to make amends, to blot out the evils of the past. (RISING) I must be strong ! (SITTING AGAIN) But I'm not ! George would never let me be. If only - (LOOKS ROUND AND SEES THE WINE) If only there was someone. (CROSSING TO SIDEBOARD AND PICKING UP WINE) I know I musn't. It's the devil's brew, but some find comfort, just a little would help - I must have something. (TAKES A GLASS FROM OUT OF SIDEBOARD AND POURS HERSELF A DRINK) It can't be so very wrong if George - only now and again - I won't be so weak when it's all over. (CROSSING BACK TO CHAIR UP CENTRE) You found it a comfort, Lettie, didn't you ? (SIPS THE WINE) Something has to help. I must be strong. Tomorrow, I'll see Mr Wilkins. They shall have it all and perhaps, dear George and Lettie, they'll begin to believe that we do understand and are not blinded by hate.

AS SHE CONTINUES TO SIP THE WINE, THE CURTAIN FALLS.

15

FURNITURE AND PROPERTY LIST

On stage: Standard lamp (practical)
             Small occasional table
             Small dining room table
             3 dining room chairs
             Telephone table   On it: a telephone
             Small sideboard   On it: a bottle of wine (opened)
                             In it: 5 wine glasses, pen and notepad,
                                        table cloth.

Off stage: Glass of water

Personal   Megan - small bottle containing water
             Merryl - stage knife

SOUND PLOT

F.X.	Doorbell	Cue:	HESTER	It's ours now; he has no use for it.
F.X.	Doorbell	Cue:	LETTIE	I'm just not strong like you.
F.X.	Phone ring	Cue	HESTER	Now go - you'll get your money.

LIGHTING PLOT

Property fittings required : working standard lamp.

Interior - living room - day but with curtains drawn.

Apparent source of light: window U.C. with drawn curtains
standard lamp D.C.

Setting to open: daylight through curtained window U.C.

Cue: HESTER   Joan, put that lamp on, will you - switch on spot
                          giving apparent light source and extra lights to
                          give full acting area light.

10
17 April
''

Committee Room